-ell as in well

Mary Elizabeth Salzmann

Consulting Editor Monica Marx, M.A./Reading Specialist

ABDO
Publishing Company

Published by SandCastle™, an imprint of ABDO Publishing Company, 4940 Viking Drive, Edina, Minnesota 55435.

Printed in the United States.

Credits
Edited by: Pam Price
Curriculum Coordinator: Nancy Tuminelly
Cover and Interior Design and Production: Mighty Media
Photo Credits: Brand X Pictures, Comstock, Corbis Images, Eyewire Images, Hemera, PhotoDisc, Stockbyte

Library of Congress Cataloging-in-Publication Data

Salzmann, Mary Elizabeth, 1968-
     -Ell as in well / Mary Elizabeth Salzmann.
          p. cm. -- (Word families. Set II)
     Summary: Introduces, in brief text and illustrations, the use of the letter combination "ell" in such words as "well," "smell," "shell," and "yell."
     ISBN 1-59197-231-0
     1. Readers (Primary) [1. Vocabulary. 2. Reading.] I. Title. II. Series.

PE1119 .S234225 2003
428.1--dc21

2002038630

SandCastle™ books are created by a professional team of educators, reading specialists, and content developers around five essential components that include phonemic awareness, phonics, vocabulary, text comprehension, and fluency. All books are written, reviewed, and leveled for guided reading, early intervention reading, and Accelerated Reader® programs and designed for use in shared, guided, and independent reading and writing activities to support a balanced approach to literacy instruction.

Let Us Know

After reading the book, SandCastle would like you to tell us your stories about reading. What is your favorite page? Was there something hard that you needed help with? Share the ups and downs of learning to read. We want to hear from you! To get posted on the ABDO Publishing Company Web site, send us e-mail at:

sandcastle@abdopub.com

SandCastle Level: Beginning

-ell Words

bell

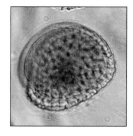

cell

shell

smell

well

yell

Kim helps ring the bell.

Ray uses a microscope
to look at a cell.

Hal holds his turtle
by its shell.

The flowers have a
nice smell.

There is a pump on this well.

Ken gives a happy yell.

Nell and the Wishing Well

One day Nell
went for a walk in the dell.

She came upon
a wishing well.

She put a coin in the well
and wished for a shell.

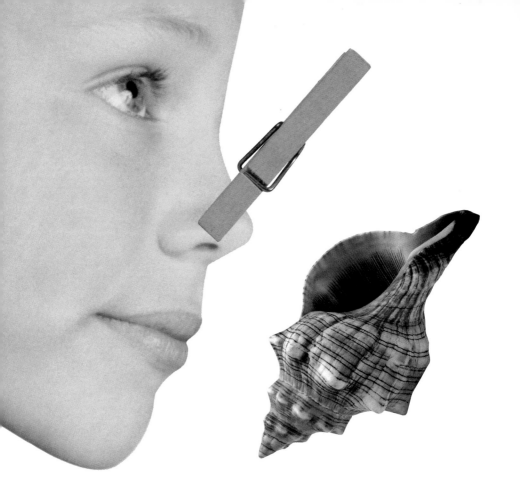

But the shell from the well
had a bad smell.

So she tried again
and wished for a bell.

"i-n-c-h"

"j-o-k-e"

"a-p-e"

"g-r-i-n"

"h-u-g"

"l-i-k-e"

"v-i-n-e"

"n-o-s-e"

"e-g-g"

But the bell wouldn't ring.
All it did was spell!

WELL

So Nell threw the shell and the bell back into the well.

Suddenly the well
started to swell!

Nell was so scared
that she gave a loud yell!

She ran home so fast
that she almost fell.

And Nell never
went back
to the well
in the dell.

The -ell Word Family

bell	sell
cell	shell
dell	smell
dwell	spell
fell	swell
jell	tell
knell	well
Nell	yell

Glossary

Some of the words in this list may have more than one meaning. The meaning listed here reflects the way the word is used in the book.

cell   a microscopic part of a person, animal, or plant

dell   a small valley

microscope   an instrument you look through to see things that are too small to see with just your eyes

pump   a device that forces liquid or gas from one place to another

swell   to grow larger

well   a deep hole that you can get water, oil, or gas from

About SandCastle™

A professional team of educators, reading specialists, and content developers created the SandCastle™ series to support young readers as they develop reading skills and strategies and increase their general knowledge. The SandCastle™ series has four levels that correspond to early literacy development in young children. The levels are provided to help teachers and parents select the appropriate books for young readers.

Emerging Readers
(no flags)

Beginning Readers
(1 flag)

Transitional Readers
(2 flags)

Fluent Readers
(3 flags)

These levels are meant only as a guide. All levels are subject to change.

To see a complete list of SandCastle™ books and other nonfiction titles from ABDO Publishing Company, visit www.abdopub.com or contact us at:

4940 Viking Drive, Edina, Minnesota 55435 • 1-800-800-1312 • fax: 1-952-831-1632